Original title:
Root Rot Riddles

Copyright © 2025 Creative Arts Management OÜ
All rights reserved.

Author: Penelope Hawthorne
ISBN HARDBACK: 978-1-80567-327-9
ISBN PAPERBACK: 978-1-80567-626-3

Chronicles of Fading Vitality

In the pot, the herbs once danced,
Now they droop, oh what a chance!
Turns out they're just too wet and shy,
Their dreams of glory now say goodbye.

A little droplet here and there,
Thought I'd help, but now I swear!
They mourn for sunlight, beg for air,
While I'm overwatering without a care.

Celestial Shadows on Earthen Grains

Beneath the soil where secrets hide,
Little roots were full of pride.
Now they quiver, they're feeling sad,
Too much love can drive them mad.

As I sprinkle, they start to cringe,
Their little faces start to singe.
"Dear gardener," they moan and sigh,
"Just a dab, don't let us fry!"

Whispers in the Underbelly

Down below, where critters play,
The roots complain about their day.
They joke of swims in too much muck,
While I just scratch my head in luck.

"I thought you liked a little rain!"
Says one root while trying to explain.
"Too much of fun can be a pain,
Now we're down here with a sore refrain."

The Fraying Threads Below

The roots are tangled, a messy plot,
Once sturdy threads, now look like rot.
They giggle low, share their fears,
Of soggy graves and soggy cheers.

"Too wet to waltz, too dry to dine,
We wrote a song, it's quite divine!"
Their brittle laughter fills the space,
In this muddy, silly rootsy race.

The Enigma of Fading Greens

The plants are waving, quite a sight,
But their leaves are drooping, what a fright!
They drink too much, like a thirsty clown,
Wondering why they're wilting down.

Their friends all giggle in the sun,
While these greens sit, feeling done.
With overzealous thirst, they've brewed their plight,
A comedy played in the fading light.

Shadows in the Underground

In the dark they whisper, roots debrief,
"Why is our party turning to grief?"
The soil is soggy, a watery pit,
"Let's find the exit, where's the wit?"

Gestures of fungi, they laugh aloud,
"Here's to the drowning, let's make it proud!"
With shovel tunes in the muddy mitt,
Roots bemuse themselves, just a bit.

Dialogues of Dying Roots

Two roots were chatting, having a spree,
"Is it just me, or are we too free?"
They spilled their secrets, both shared a sigh,
"I think we're sinking, oh me, oh my!"

One said, "My friend, we've had too much rain,
This party's great, but it's causing us pain!"
Their laughter echoed through the damp ground,
Roots in a tangle, humor unbound.

The Mystery of Soggy Souls

Once there were greens that loved a splash,
In puddles of water, they made quite a crash.
But too much of joy turned to despair,
Now they float like boats in a soggy fair.

Tales of unease, they quickly spread,
"Leave it to us, we'll float instead!"
With sarcasm sprouting in their leafy shoe,
They joke as they drown, just a humorous view.

Threads of Time Beneath the Ground

In the soil, secrets twine,
Little worms dream and dine.
Spinning tales of what they find,
Tangled mess, oh so unkind!

Tangled roots play hide and seek,
Whispering jokes, how unique!
Gnarly knots and twists, oh dear,
Nature's riddle's loud and clear!

The Wistful Weaving of Roots

Roots like fingers in a race,
Grasp at air, they're in a chase.
Bumping into stones with glee,
'Oops, excuse me! Can't you see?'

They weave a tapestry of fun,
Trying hard to block the sun.
Riddles lie in every twist,
While critters dance and coexist!

Beneath the Blossoms, Darkness Lurks

Under petals, shadows laugh,
Roots conspire, do the math.
'One plus one, oh look—a mess!'
They tangle 'round with pure finesse!

Blossoms giggle, roots complain,
'Why'd you step on our domain?'
A burrow here, a snicker there,
In this chaos, who would care?

The Enigma of Nature's Toll

Nature's game, a puzzle wide,
With roots that play, and stones that slide.
'Is it spring? Or just my shoe?'
Jokes pop up, as fungi do!

So here we stand, beneath the boughs,
Roots scratching heads, making vows.
To solve the riddle, join the fun,
Where nature dances, and all is won!

Secrets Beneath the Soil

In the dark, the worms do dance,
While tiny roots play their chance.
A little bug with a sly grin,
Gobbles up what's left within.

Mysterious whispers, oh so slight,
A secret party in the night.
Each little sprout, with tales to share,
Of how they're missing their proper care.

Whispers of the Withering

A wilted leaf hangs low with pride,
Complaining softly, it can't hide.
The silly flower, in a huff,
Says watering twice is just too tough!

Beneath the ground, a gossip spree,
With roots exchanging glee, you'll see.
They laugh and roll, a funky bunch,
Pretending they're not in a crunch.

Decay's Silent Puzzle

Consider the life of the muddy trail,
Where fungal friends are far from frail.
They giggle and plot in the shadowy dark,
While the clueless bulbs lurk, still without spark.

A riddle unfolds from the loamy earth,
Creating chaos, and yet—what mirth!
Each droopy stem is part of the game,
As they raise their heads, trying to claim fame.

Beneath the Surface: A Hidden Tale

In the dirt where secrets grow,
Little roots put on a show.
Laughing softly, they twist and twine,
Wondering why they can't sip wine.

The soil chuckles, a playful prank,
As moisture runs down the fishy tank.
With every sip, they tease and jest,
While leaves complain they're never blessed.

Fables From the Forgotten Depths

In a pot where plants once thrived,
Now the soil feels like a dive.
Little worms threw a wild spree,
Said, "We're couch potatoes, can't you see?"

One small fern had a grand dream,
To bloom bright, or at least to gleam.
But mud told jokes, it couldn't bear,
"Oh, leaf it be, we're quite a pair!"

The daisies danced, but lost their chance,
In muddy puddles, they tried to prance.
"Water us less!" the violets cried,
"Or drown us all where we can't hide!"

So bet on roots with a watchful eye,
For deep in dirt, snickers lie.
A tale of giggles from fellows unfit,
In the deep where soggy plants sit.

A Symphony of Wilted Stems

Oh, the sad brassica, once full of cheer,
Now drooping low, it sheds a tear.
"I'm a wilted star in this leafy show,
And I can't find where the good vibes flow!"

The carrots sighed, "We're striking it rich,
In this heavy muck, we seem to sit!
Our dreams of being crisp and bright,
Turned into mush by the dark of night!"

A tiny thistle called with a grin,
"Let's have a giggle, we lose, we win!
With every droop, we share a song,
In this funny fate, we all belong!"

They laughed through gloom, oh what a jest,
Rooted together, they felt the best.
A symphony played from below the ground,
Where every wilted stem has fun abound.

The Lament of Lost Nourishment

Once a garden filled with delight,
Now it's a horror, a comical sight.
"Where's the sunshine?" the herbs do complain,
As they wiggle their roots in a soggy bane.

The tomatoes trip over their own vines,
Saying, "We're lost in these mud-stained lines!"
They long for a feast of soil so grand,
But sogginess plots a sneaky plan.

Basil dreams of a savory charm,
But moisture creeps in, raising alarm.
"I can't taste the pizza!" he shouts with dread,
"Make me a salad or I'll end up dead!"

With silly rhymes and murmurs sweet,
The garden laughs, though feeling beat.
For even loss in nourishment's plight,
Can spark joy and giggles, day or night.

The Depths of Despair

In the soil so deep, where logic goes low,
The roots all ponder their woeful show.
"Did we misstep in our quest for space?
Or maybe we danced at the wrong pace?"

The ferns fret over bumpy trails,
While daisies spin tales of cocktail fails.
The peppers ponder their fate in gloom,
"Send down some sunshine, keep us in bloom!"

With every drip from the clouds above,
Came a flood of stories, no hint of love.
"Let's chuckle through this soggy strife,"
For in muddy mischief, they find their life!

As the garden gurgles with laughter once more,
In the depths of despair, they ignite the floor.
Roots wriggling in rhythm, a humor parade,
Turns sadness to giggles in the green charade.

The Grave of Unseen Abandonment

In the soil, where dreams decay,
A plant stood tall, then lost its way.
With whispers of hope, it spread its wings,
But the plot twist stings like a bee with stings.

Under leaves that had turned to dust,
A gardener sighed, "Oh, this was a bust."
For every weed, a snicker and laugh,
Who knew plant care could spark such a gaffe?

The Skeletal Remains of Growth

Amidst the graves of greenery wilted,
Stand the remains, all hope jilted.
A cactus complained, 'I thirst for the sun!'
But in this plot, it's all just done.

With roots like spaghetti, all tangled and mad,
The plants plot revenge, 'This is just sad!'
They chuckle softly, in shadows they lie,
'Next time, we'll party, just watch us spry!'

Lullabies for Lost Landscapes

Sleep, dear plants, in your grave of gloom,
The bumblebee hums a dirge in the room.
With fingers in soil, the gardener sighs,
As weeds tell tales with mischievous eyes.

In the moonlight, they murmur their fears,
"My leaves were vibrant, now filled with tears."
Yet in this chaos, laughter does bloom,
As composted dreams dance in the gloom.

Filaments of Forgotten Lies

Once lush and green, now just a joke,
A sprout had dreams, then it must have broke.
It whispered sweet nothings to the stars,
Only to find it had planted in jars.

The gardener chuckled, "Just water it, friend!"
But those poor leaves knew they'd meet their end.
In filaments tangled, they spun their plight,
Claiming, "Next year, we'll really take flight!"

Multitudes Burdened in the Mud

In the garden, plants all frown,
With their feet stuck in the brown.
Wiggly worms, they laugh and tease,
"Who needs legs when you can squeeze?"

Sunflowers bend with heads held low,
As puddles whisper, "What a show!"
The daisies giggle, roots so stout,
But it's muddy mayhem all about!

Traces of Trouble Underground

Down below where critters scurry,
The roots are panicked, oh so blurry.
"Is that a smell?" the tulips cry,
"Or just more water? Oh, my my!"

The carrots chuckle in their lair,
Wishing for sunshine, is it fair?
With every drop, they seem to drown,
As earthworms spin without a frown!

Vignettes of Vanishing Vitality

Petunias sulk in shadowy clumps,
While daisies bubble with watery grumps.
"Did you see that?" a daffodil shouts,
"Life's just a joke when it's full of sprout doubts!"

Beneath the surface, what a mess,
Giggling roots in their soggy dress.
Laughing as they lose their zest,
Who knew mud could be such a jest?

Compositions of Concealed Decline

In the soil where secrets creep,
Roots go to play and sometimes sleep.
"Is this our fate?" the tulips moan,
"Just dreams of flowers that aren't our own?"

With muddy shoes, the weeds all dance,
While blossoms ponder a blooming chance.
In this comedy of green despair,
They laugh at life, with roots laid bare!

Petals That Speak of Pain

Petals droop, all sad and torn,
They whisper tales of plants forlorn.
With hopes to bloom, they tried their best,
Yet ended up just like the rest.

Wishing for sunshine, and oh, some rain,
Instead, they soaked in a puddle of pain.
A soil bath sounded like a treat,
But now they're feeling quite off-beat.

With dirt on their leaves, they wear a frown,
Their leafy dreams are merely brown.
Yet every sprout still shares their worth,
With laughter found beneath the earth.

The Lingering Memory of Growth

In gardens bright where flowers thrived,
Are memories of green that's now deprived.
Roots reminiscing, a tale so tall,
Of moments shared before the fall.

Glimmers of glory in bright sunlight,
Now fade to whispers in the night.
With secret giggles and shifty sighs,
The soil now hides a million lies.

Each tender sprout was once so proud,
But now they mope beneath the cloud.
Though growth's a laugh, it comes with strains,
And laughter echoes through the plains.

Remnants of the Silent Struggle

Once there was a stalk so bold,
It stood so tall, or so I'm told.
But whispers came of hidden woes,
Beneath the ground, the struggle grows.

A tangle here, a knotty twist,
A fight for space that can't be missed.
They chuckle low, those roots in fright,
In muddy battles, they lose the light.

What once was bloom is now a jest,
A lovely mess, but who can guess?
In hushed tones, they share their fears,
In laughter's glow, they shift their gears.

Dance of the Delicate Roots

Oh, what a dance beneath the ground,
Where roots twirl fast without a sound.
They wiggle and jiggle with such delight,
In the dark, they groove into the night.

One toe in mud, the other in air,
These tricky dancers live without a care.
They whisper jokes, share their woes,
In this wild game, anything goes!

When clumps get tangled, hearts race a beat,
In nature's ball-off, who claims defeat?
Yet through the fuss and giddy spins,
The dance goes on, and laughter wins.

A Melody of Earth's Lament

In soil where dreams once thrived,
Droopy leaves now come alive.
Wiggly worms hold hands in grief,
While fungi dance, a mischief's chief.

"Why so sad?" the daisies cry,
As puddles form beneath the sky.
With roots that twist in tangled glee,
They question, 'What happened to me?'

But ants just chuckle, busy on their way,
Roaming through what the plants betray.
In the muck, the laughter swells,
For even mud can spin its tales!

So twirl and giggle, let the garden sway,
In every squishy spot, there's joy at play.
Let's toast to roots who've lost their fight,
And share a laugh in morning light.

The Tragedy of Stifled Growth

The carrots sulk beneath the ground,
Whispers of sorrow all around.
With dreams of salad, crisp and bright,
Now creeping molds are their plight.

A cabbage stares, its head held low,
"We're stuck in this soggy show!"
Complaining onions start to pout,
While laughing peas just hop about.

"Oh dear," says corn, "we're wet and sad,
With so much water, it feels all bad!"
Yet critters munch without a care,
In muddy games that fill the air.

So raise a toast with muddy froth,
To the roots who sank and swore to cloth.
In every squish, a giggle blooms,
For even muck can hold its fumes!

The Yawn of the Forgotten Ground

Here lies the soil, a sleepy heap,
Underneath, the critters creep.
With roots that sigh and gently yawn,
The days stretch out, the nights are drawn.

Potatoes grumble, "Get us out!"
While sleepy grass gives a slouching shout.
"Can someone please start a parade?"
As whispering weeds begin to fade.

With every droplet, they feel like clowns,
Caked in mud, adorned in frowns.
Yet, giggly grubs plan a grand escape,
Trading tales of a leafy cape.

So let them dance in jiggly glee,
For in the muck, it's fun to be!
A joyful jolt beneath the ground,
Where laughter blooms, profound, unbound!

Shivers of Life's Hidden Strains

In gardens where the veggies dance,
A little bug took a slimy chance.
He wiggles and wriggles, plotting a game,
But little did he know, it's all rather lame.

The lettuce twitches, gives a strange sigh,
While carrots giggle as they all lie.
A drama unfolds, oh what a sight,
As whispers of soil create quite a fright!

A pinecone fell, and the worms took a bow,
As laughter erupted, it's chaos now!
Little sprouts jest as they try to take root,
Unearthed hilarity in nature's pursuit.

So if you fear what hides underground,
Just chuckle a bit, it's all silly sound.
For nature's a jester in floral disguise,
With jokes that tickle and wisdom that flies.

The Tear of Nature's Pulse

A daisy cried out, 'Oh woe is me!'
My petals are droopy, so slouchy, you see.
But a dandelion laughed with a puff and a cheer,
'Quit all your whining, just let it be clear!'

The clouds in the sky, they giggled so bright,
As raindrops fell down, a shimmering light.
Each drop had a joke, a punchline to share,
Making puddles laugh, while flowers laid bare.

'Why did the cactus refuse to feel blue?'
'Because it was prickly and stuck like a glue!'
The sentinels chuckled in their spiny embrace,
While critters hopped by, a foam, silly race.

So when you sense nature's sweet pulse all around,
Know joy is concealed in each smile unbound.
Let laughter erupt where the green shoots abound,
For tears of the earth bring humor profound.

The Obscured Dialogues of Dearth

In whispering fields where shadows creep,
The pumpkins plot secrets they can't keep.
The corn stalks gossip with a rustling glee,
And beans snicker softly behind the old tree.

A moth with a monocle, wise as can be,
Proclaims to the turnips, 'Just wait and you'll see!'
While onions hold court, crying soft tears,
Claiming they've witnessed a thousand dark years.

An acorn replied, 'Now don't be absurd!'
The truth about life is often unheard.
They chuckled and snorted, shared tales of their past,
While seeds of hope gathered the courage to last.

So heed not the whispers of what lies beneath,
For laughter and joy, they are risking a sheath.
In the depths of the earth, the humor resides,
In the whispers of life where the wittiness hides.

Flowers of Reflection in the Deep

Beneath the soil, where giggles reside,
Blooming in silence, they take life in stride.
Roses debate 'who's the fairest of all,'
While violets chime in, 'We're tiny but tall!'

A sunflower stood, with a cheeky grin,
Saying, 'I'm the tallest, and that's how I win!'
While daisies exchanged some witty retorts,
Declaring the grass had the best of all thoughts.

In secret, the roots threw a carnival show,
Where worms wore top hats, all ready to go.
With laughter erupting from everywhere near,
The plants' hidden lives bring more joy than fear.

So dive into gardens, where stories are spun,
Where flowers reflect, and the fun's just begun.
For in every petal, and each teetering leaf,
Lies a comedy of nature, to banish your grief.

The Unraveling of Verdant Dreams

In a pot so snug and neat,
A plant was sure it had it beat.
But whispers came from below,
'You won't believe the soil show!'

The roots danced in a muddy spree,
With giggles like a bumblebee.
They tossed their woes, they twirled around,
And laughed at leaves that lost their crown.

Oh, how the petals drooped and sighed,
Misguided dreams, they tried to hide.
Yet every leaf in disarray,
Would joke of better, sunny days!

So here's to plants with dreams so wild,
Who twirl in fate like a playful child.
Though tangled fates may pull them down,
Their laughter still will wear the crown.

Tales of Faded Florals

In a garden full of cheer,
Faded petals shed a tear.
'What happened to your vibrant glow?'
'We fancied deep-water flow!'

With roots submerged in desperate plight,
They longed for warmth, but lost the fight.
'Oh dear friends, we tried to swim,
But now we drift, it's kind of grim!'

The daisies laughed, the lilies cheered,
While roses sighed, for dreams they steered.
'Next time, let's stick to the ground,
Or find a beach where joy is found!'

So remember, when in despair,
The floral tales of foolish air.
For every bloom that met its end,
Can teach a lesson, or just a blend!

Shadows in the Earthen Embrace

Beneath the soil, so dark and deep,
Lurks a party, can't hear a peep.
The roots invite the bugs for fun,
While soil creeps whisper, 'Yeah, let's run!'

The shadows jiggle, the soil shakes,
A wild fiesta that no one makes!
Little critters join the row,
What's that? Oh, just a worm's show!

Yet when the sun shines overhead,
The dance turns weird—oh, what a dread!
With drooping leaves and disheveled stems,
They ponder if they'll be cool again!

But laughter fills the earthy gloom,
Even shadows find a room.
So, dance away till daylight breaks,
And wallow in some wiggly wakes!

Beneath the Surface: A Tormented Tale

Beneath the surface, a tale unfolds,
With roots in chaos, their fate so bold.
A pot of dreams turned soggy mess,
Where water jesters jest and stress!

They squabbled hard for a sip of sun,
Each leaf a player, jokes on the run.
One roots cried out, 'I'm sinking fast!'
While others cheered, 'Make fun, at last!'

They gathered round for a joke or two,
On tangled mischief, they grew askew.
'We shouldn't drink so deep, it's true!
Next time, let's stick with just a dew!'

In every drop that soaked their plight,
Was laughter born of silly fright.
For plants who jested with wet despair,
Found joy in muck, a quagmire rare!

When Nutrients Whisper Goodbye

In the soil, whispers stray,
Nutrients packing up for a holiday.
Roots are confused, feel so low,
Sipping air like it's the show.

Plants huddle, sharing cringe,
"Did we forget to water, or binge?"
They argue, leaves flutter in the breeze,
"Let's send the nutrients a 'please!'"

Sun's shining bright, they try to beam,
But without a meal, it's a meme.
A garden party lacking the feast,
With weeds as guests, it's a real beast!

As the roots withdraw in despair,
A garden clown appears with flair.
"You're all invited, let's have some fun!
Who wants to dance? Oh wait, just run!"

The Murmur of Neglected Life

In shadows deep, life starts to moan,
Plants whisper secrets to the stone.
Roots are dreaming of a grand escape,
While leaves are shouting, "Get some tape!"

A wilted bloom wrinks its face,
"I think we've lost the watering race!"
Nearby, a cactus cracks a joke,
"Hey friend, you look like a bad yolk!"

Bugs throw a party at the base,
While saplings wonder about their grace.
"Can we call for help?" a petal squeaks,
But all that answers are the creeks.

They laugh at the storm clouds' frown,
"Let's toast to the veggies, down!"
A banquet of weeds flows like a stream,
In the garden, reality feels like a dream!

Puzzle of the Fading Flora

A plant on a quest for the sunny spot,
But the sun's kind of shy, what a plot!
Leaves flip through a botanical book,
"Maybe a soil facelift is what we took!"

Roots are playing hide and seek,
"Where's the water? I can't feel my cheek!"
A daisy sighs, "I'm losing my charm,
With fungus creeping, it's raising alarm!"

The garden gnomes start to conspire,
"Let's set up a festival, let's ignite fire!"
With a wink, they sing, "We'll dance and cheer,
For each wilted bloom we hold dear!"

With laughter ringing, the weeds all join,
They'll riddle life, make it a coin!
A playful secret, a garden's sophistry,
All is well, in this green tapestry!

Buried Dilemmas in the Garden

Beneath the earth, a drama unfolds,
Roots in meetings, sharing old woes.
"Could it be us?" one petal quips,
"Or did that compost take too many trips?"

A daffodil sighs, "So much neglect,
When flowers collude, who earns respect?"
Grass blades snicker, "Come join the fun,
It's all about the sun, you'll come undone!"

From the depths, the secrets cry,
As worms dissolve like they're tasting pie.
"Water's our princess, can't you tell?
Without her splendor, we're under a spell!"

In this muddy riddle, giggles collide,
A cheer for the blooms! It's a wild ride.
They'll dance with the breeze till the day is done,
In the puzzling garden, life's still so fun!

Descent into the Darkened Loam

In the earth where secrets creep,
Little roots take a dive so deep.
They giggle as they wiggle and spin,
But someone's not wearing a grin!

Neighbors argue and twist in plight,
"Why is your hair turning brown at night?"
One plant cries, "This is quite absurd!"
"Don't blame me, it's all the worms!"

Down in the dirt, they plot and scheme,
Dreaming of water, they make a team.
But oh, the giggles turn to fear,
When soggy friends start drawing near!

So next time your roots feel the doom,
Just laugh it off, and lighten the gloom.
For in the soil, madness may bloom,
A comedy show in the darkened room!

Agonizing Entanglement of Essence

Twisted roots with tangled tales,
Whispering woes of soggy trails.
"I can't find my flip-flop!" one did yell,
While another was stuck in a marigold shell.

"Stop stepping on me," a root did shout,
As potting soil laughed and danced about.
They aimed for freedom but missed the mark,
Instead, they sunk deeper in the park.

"A little space, please, I beg you dear!
I don't want your mildew cling so near!"
But wriggly worms joined the tangled mess,
Saying, "Fellow roots, we're in this stress!"

Let this be a lesson, oh wise green friends,
Sometimes together is where the fun ends.
So next time you feel a squeeze or a bind,
Remember the laughter that's hard to find!

The Roots that Cried for Help

Oh roots, they sighed, "What is this fate?
We're trapped in muck, it's far too late!"
"I swear I saw light," one root did squeal,
"Above this damp, it must be surreal!"

With vines entwined, they gossiped low,
"Do you think it's too late to go with the flow?"
They tried to wiggle, they tried to sway,
But mud was thicker than a fruitcake's stay!

"Hey you, up there, can you hear our plea?
We need a lifeguard, so set us free!"
But the gardener just chuckled in glee,
"Grow a little longer, just wait and see!"

So when you see roots, down in despair,
Remember their giggles still linger there.
For while they may cry in a feathery heap,
They'll rise again, dreams rooting deep!

Spirit of the Crumbling Substratum

Deep in the dirt where the spirits hide,
Lived a lonely root named Clyde.
He'd giggle and wiggle, with one last laugh,
Dancing through mud like a sassy giraffe.

"Oh no, oh dear, it's getting too wet,
Will I get eaten? I'm not ready yet!"
But crumbling soil just shimmied with cheer,
"Come on, dear Clyde, we'll conquer your fear!"

With every squish, they'd play hide and seek,
"Is that a raindrop or a funny beak?"
Together they morphed into laughter and fun,
Twisting and tumbling under the sun.

So heed, little roots, with a joke or two,
Even crumbling ground can sparkle for you.
For every puddle of gloom that you find,
Can be a laugh fest, if you're rooted in kind!

Fragmented Lives in the Earth

Half a tomato on a trowel,
Grumbled loudly, "Life's a trial!"
Worms chuckled, 'What a sight!'
Eating salad day and night.

A cactus weeps, 'I'm feeling pale,'
"Don't complain!" says a potted snail.
The thorns all laugh, the soil shakes,
Jokes about garden stakes and flakes.

Celestial Dreams Interred

A daisy dreams of space and stars,
Giggling lightly with the jars.
"Pretend you're brave!" said the herb,
While a worm claimed, "I'm a superb!"

The moon peeks in with a wink,
While flowers ponder, stop and think.
Can they rise up to the sky?
Life below can make you fly!

The Slumbering Echoes Below

A mushroom snores, oh what a sound,
Down in the dark where roots abound.
"Wake me later!" it did boast,
As critters danced and made a toast.

A beetle rolled its shiny ball,
Claiming, "I'm the strongest of all!"
The soil buzzed and cracks revealed,
The laughter hidden, roots concealed.

The Fate of Forgotten Foliage

A leaf lay flat, it felt so blue,
It couldn't find a friend or two.
"To the compost I shall go!"
The laughter rose, "You put on quite the show!"

A flower sighed, "I used to bloom,"
Now hoarding secrets in the gloom.
With tangled tales from days of yore,
They chuckled at the tales of sore.

Echoes of Entangled Life

In the garden so bright and cheery,
Leaves dance, but their roots look weary.
A tangle of fibers, oh what a mess!
Who knew that plants could feel such stress?

Twirled around like they're playing a game,
Whispers of soil call out each name.
'Hey, you over there, have you seen my drink?'
Roots shout aloud, 'We're starting to sink!'

With laughter afloat in the warm, sweet air,
They joke about life, and the burdens they bear.
"Let's grab a cuppa," one root will declare,
"While we ponder why it's so hard to share!"

Through the tangled mess, the humor explodes,
For even in chaos, the laughter erodes.
So cheers to the roots, who bring joy in strife,
In their entangled dance, we find true life.

The Soil's Silent Lament

Deep in the dirt, a secret confides,
The soil hums softly, where laughter resides.
"I have the best roots, but they're all intertwined,
Oh, what a circus! How did we wind?"

"Just yesterday, I felt quite spry,
Now I'm the punchline, oh, how I sigh!
Too many pals crammed all around,
We're fighting for space in this underground."

Sprouts giggle, weaving in and out,
What's the best way to avoid a pout?
They share their stories, each twist and turn,
Of how they're trying not to squirm and churn.

So here's a toast, to struggle and play,
In the world of plants, we find our way.
With soil and roots, we'll laugh and thrive,
In our earthy home, we're truly alive!

A Tangle of Tendrils

Oh, a tangle of tendrils, what a sight!
Big stems in a jumble, trying to take flight.
"Excuse me, dear neighbor, you're crowding my space,
Could you shift just a bit? I'm losing my grace!"

"Not a chance!" replies with a wink and a grin,
"I'm cozy right here, let the fun begin!
We'll twist and we'll turn, it's a root party now,
No worries at all, just let go and wow!"

Leaves chuckle softly, what a planty surprise!
For laughter comes easy with these leafy guys.
"How'd we get tangled, in this wicked dance?"
"Well, I blame the sun; it led us to prance!"

So, they settle in snug, this whimsical crew,
With stories and giggles, they'll see it all through.
In the garden's embrace, they'll weather the storm,
In this tangle of life, they're always warm.

The Puzzles of Planted Dreams

Beneath the earth, the dreams unfold,
In shadowy whispers, their secrets are told.
"Is that your stem? I thought it was mine!"
"Oh dear, let's not bicker; life's too divine!"

A riddle of roots, winding every way,
"Can we map this madness? Should we even stay?"
A sprout with ambition says, "I'll lead the tour,
You won't need a map; it's all a big score!"

So they frolic through loam, as friends do align,
Discovering twists in the roots of the vine.
With laughter a plenty, they tackle each to-do,
For life in the soil is a puzzling brew.

And when night comes softly, they share a deep cheer,
In this charming chaos, they shed every fear.
So toast to the plants, who dream down below,
Together they flourish, together they grow!

Dreaming of a World Reclaimed

In gardens lush where veggies bloat,
They dream of life in a plastic boat.
With roots so clean, they sing and sway,
Yet down below, they're in dismay.

A squirrel glance, with mischief grins,
Unknowing the woe of their leafy sins.
They whisper low of a grand parade,
While all their roots come softly frayed.

Around the pots, the compost swells,
With hidden jokes that only it tells.
Oh, leafy pals in sun's warm ray,
You laugh as you grow—come what may!

So raise a glass with soil on hand,
To every plant from our funny land.
Reclaimed dreams, with laughter loud,
Let victory sprout, oh brave, proud crowd!

Enchanted Whispers in the Earth

Beneath the ground, the critters plot,
In a silly game, the wise worms trot.
With hidden giggles, they share a fate,
While sprouts above debate their state.

A snail in shoes, so ready to race,
Calls out to the buds, 'Let's win this chase!'
With petals bright, they leap and prance,
Unknowing of the mud's sly dance.

In shadows deep, the fungi cheer,
As roots do twist, they give a sneer.
'This game of growth is quite absurd,
Yet here we are, without a word!'

Under the earth, a party sways,
With sizable glee on a rooty fray.
Whispers so sweet, from underground kin,
Creating joy where all begin.

Soliloquy of the Sorrowful Soil

Oh weary ground, with tales to share,
You spill your secrets with gentle care.
While flowers above dance with delight,
The earth, in silence, sighs through the night.

A rock grumbles loud, overrated fame,
"Hear my woes!" it starts the same.
With every turn, a mystery unfolds,
As roots and dirt exchange their golds.

In the soggy depths, a dark joke stirs,
With tangled roots with no 'for hers'!
"What's life?" cries one with leafy crest,
"Just silly games in this dirty quest."

Yet laughter echoes, beneath tangled beds,
Of joyous whispers where no one treads.
So soil, dear friend, take pride in your role,
For without your fate, we'd miss the whole.

Embrace of the Wounded Underworld

In the dark corners where whispers roam,
The underworld's got its own sweet home.
With roots entangled, an awkward embrace,
Life's funny misfit in this crowded space.

A chipmunk frowns, with a faux pas grin,
"How to plant something that won't wear thin?"
While bulbs plot mischief beneath the clay,
Painting their plans in a subtle way.

Down in the depth, the worms conspire,
"Let's throw a ball and set the mire!"
So all the sprouts join the grand affair,
And giggles bubble up through the air.

Together they dance in this muddled fun,
While oak trees chuckle in the warming sun.
In jests of soil, riches shall twine,
For even in struggle, we flourish divine!

Riddles in the Rooted Realm

In the garden's shadow, weeds conspire,
With secrets buried, they'll never tire.
Each twist of a vine, a tale to tell,
Of thirsty roots that think they're swell.

The carrots chuckle, the onions jest,
"We're safe from trouble, we're simply blessed!"
Yet down below, the true comedy lies,
As roots grab for snacks, and laughter flies!

A sneaky old bug, with quite the plan,
Cracks jokes on leaves, a merry man.
But every punchline, it turns to leer,
As roots shake with giggles, or is that fear?

So come for a visit, the soil's alive,
Where laughter and chaos and mischief thrive.
In the hidden world, beneath the green dome,
You'll find it's a party, far away from home.

Whispering Woes Beneath the Soil

Deep down below, the critters conspire,
With whispers of woes that never tire.
A potato sighed, as he peeked out wide,
"I can't stay here, it's way too inside!"

A fungus once joked, with a cheeky grin,
"Why fit in soil when you can spin?"
But roots in despair thought it was a bust,
As laughter turned sour, and they moved in rust.

The earthworms laughed, in their wriggly dance,
"We're the main act in this garden prance!"
But when roots heard it, they started to mope,
"Are we just the stage, without any hope?"

So tune in, dear friend, to the chatter below,
Where funny and funky, the tales start to flow.
In the earth's tucked whispers, a giggle, a snort,
A riddle of roots in an underground sport!

Secrets of the Withering Undergrowth

In the undergrowth thick, where secrets unfold,
The roots tell their stories, both witty and bold.
A rose sighed, "Why do weeds like to prance?"
As they danced 'round the daisies in a wild romance.

"Let's have a debate, here's my grand idea!"
The roots argued back, "Oh dear, oh dear!"
A bumblebee buzzed, brought a jar of jam,
"Let's make a truce, or we'll all be spam!"

Down low, where the sunlight barely creeps,
The lilies rolled eyes, as the laughter leaps.
"Why can't we all share and just get along?"
But the roots just snickered, saying, "Not yet! Hang on!"

Through roots and through shoots, the jokes never fade,
As blooms bloom in chorus, a vibrant parade.
With mysteries tangled, in fun we'll engage,
In the world of the withering, we turn a fresh page.

Shadows of Decay in the Dark Earth

In shadows we twirl, where the soil is thick,
A riddle for roots, it forms quite the trick.
A cabbage cried out, with much dismay,
"Did anyone see my cabbage sway?"

The beet laughed aloud, then covered his mouth,
"You're dancing alone, down here in the south!"
But all were so busy, in their tangled play,
They forgot all the sprouts that were going astray.

The branches overhead shared a curious scheme,
A game of hide and seek, a root's wild dream.
"Who'll find my way out?" asked Mr. Snap,
As he clung to the dirt, feeling quite flat.

So if you should wander back to this place,
Where shadows and laughter leave a bright trace,
Remember dear buddy, that roots are quite wry,
In the secrets of soil, they're the jesters who fly!

The Silent Descent of Tender Roots

In the garden, under soil's splay,
Little roots dance the day away.
Some sing soft songs of gentle cheer,
While others just sulk, drinking their beer!

A mystery brews beneath the ground,
What mischief awaits, yet to be found?
They wiggle and giggle, causing a stir,
Maybe they're planning to start a new fur!

The soil chuckles, it knows their plight,
As they tumble and stumble in late night light.
With worms as their audience, they put on a show,
The roots twist in laughter, soaking the glow!

So if you hear giggles from way down below,
Just know those roots are putting on a show.
Their silent descent, a comical jest,
As they cuddle and huddle in their cozy nest.

Enigmas of the Dying Green

Why do the leaves wear such a frown?
Their neighbors are laughing, never down.
With wilting sass and droopy grace,
They ponder their life in this leafy race.

Blooming buds whisper, 'What gives them woes?'
'A sip of good rain or just one more dose?'
The answer remains, like a game of charades,
As the daisies clutch their delicate blades.

In shadows, a tale of humor unfolds,
Spirited greens and mischievous molds.
Their riddles are funny, but how can we tell?
If plants have a hotline, they've certainly fell!

Giggles erupt like blossoms in spring,
What secrets they hold, let's dance and sing.
The dying greens ponder this puzzling scene,
In the garden of jest, where all is serene.

Beneath the Surface: A Tangle of Truth

Beneath the surface, they twist and intertwine,
Roots sharing secrets over sips of fine wine.
Yet some are lost, unsure of their goal,
Swapping old tales of folly and coal.

The tuber thinks it's far too grand,
While the fibrous crew just shakes their hand.
A jumbled mess of laughter and glee,
As they spin yarns of the old tree's decree.

With every tangle, a giggle does break,
Showing the truth can be quite the mistake.
Roots exploding with joy, in their whimsical plight,
Underneath the dirt, they party all night!

So if you dig deep, and hear their mirth,
Know the roots are joyful, celebrating their birth.
A tangle of truth in this underground maze,
With laughter unfurling in the verdant haze.

Frail Connections in the Hidden Depths

In hidden depths, connections frail,
Roots share whispers like a funny tale.
A twist here, a knot there, oh what a mess!
They giggle at branches, their leafy excess!

The carrots complain of their close-knit friends,
'We're tangled this way, when will it end?'
The beets roll their eyes, as they dig and twirl,
A dance of the underground, a weird little whirl.

With every nudge and oh-so-shy sneeze,
The roots have a party, all eager to please.
Their connections grow frail, but spirits arise,
As they plot and they scheme, beneath grassy skies.

So when you wander the garden, take heed,
Listen for laughter, it's rooted indeed!
For in those connections, both funny and strange,
Are tales of the soil, always ready to change.

The Lament of a Shattered Network

A plant sat down to have a chat,
About its friends, both flat and fat.
"My leaves feel heavy, like bad jokes,
Maybe it's my soil, filled with hoax!"

With roots that whisper tales of woe,
It plotted schemes to stay aglow.
"But here I am, all stuck in gloom,
Wishing I had taken up a broom!"

Secrets Uncovered in the Grit

In dirt so deep, where secrets dwell,
A gnome once told a curious spell.
"Don't water me too much, or you'll find,
I'm ready for a splash of thyme!"

The carrots giggled, in a row,
"Is it too late to put on a show?
We've got a tale about a blight,
But no one's here to hear our fright!"

Entwined in Solitude: A Green Elegy

A vine once moaned, with tangled wear,
"I peeked out, but saw no one there.
My friends have turned, to mush and mire,
Is solitude a plant's desire?"

With tendrils crossed, it sighed a breath,
"In leafless luck, I flirt with death.
Yet still I laugh, in this green space,
For who can frown in nature's place?"

Beneath the Skin of the Earth

Beneath the skin where whispers hide,
A worm confessed, not very wide.
"Why do they fuss, about decay?
It's just my diet, can't they play?"

The thorns agreed with frantic glee,
"Life's a puzzle, don't you see?
With every drip and every drop,
We dance around the final flop!"

The Fate of Lost Connections

In the garden, wires tangled,
Electric friends, now all mangled.
Messages sent, but never received,
Petunias sigh, their hearts deceived.

Deep in the soil, Wi-Fi's a myth,
Signal drops like a jolly old whiff.
Bees buzz loudly, but can't join in,
The party of blooms feels like a sin.

Roots and wires had a grand fight,
Fungi laughing, what a silly sight.
They'll text and vine, till the end of days,
Forgotten chats, in vibrant arrays.

Nextdoor neighbors whisper with glee,
"Is our connection doomed to be?"
Yet through the dirt and muck they grin,
For laughter sprouts from where they've been.

Haunting of the Hidden Garden

In the shade where shadows creep,
There lies a garden, secrets to keep.
Ghostly weeds with a laugh so sly,
Come out to dance when no one's nigh.

Petunias chuckle, roses jive,
As ghoulish critters come alive.
"Who watered us?" they ask with dread,
"Perhaps our dreams have all just fled!"

Compost bins sing a tune so eerie,
While moles plot mischief, oh so cheery.
Grimy gnomes peek from behind a fern,
"Mischief's afoot! Let's take our turn!"

But gardeners come with shovels and spades,
Banishing phantoms, making charades.
Yet in the night, whispers still float,
In the hidden garden where laughter's remote.

The Heartbreak Beneath the Blooms

A daisy sighs, "Love's gone awry,"
In the patch where fading petals lie.
Once a bouquet, now a single stem,
Heartache is messy; oh, which whim?

Tulips tremble with tales untold,
"Why did he leave when the sun was bold?"
Butterflies flit, with gossip divine,
"Mourning blooms take too much wine!"

Forget-me-nots weep, "What did we miss?"
In the garden, nothing's amiss.
But pollen rushes, on love's express,
For blooms will giggle, what a hot mess!

So when petals fall like tears on ground,
Remember the laughter that once was found.
For in heartbreak's grip, grows a grin,
Where roots entwined, new love can begin.

Burgeoning Safeguards of Life

In the vegetable patch, a fortress stands,
With leafy guardians and happy bands.
"Protect the sprouts!" shouts over ripe corn,
As critters gather, all accurst and worn.

Carrots don armor, radishes cheer,
Tomatoes hide underneath a veneer.
"Keep them safe from the feasting night!"
Squeaks a critter, full of fright.

With cunning traps of twine and string,
The garden defenders plot their spring.
Yet mischief rises with the setting sun,
As each vegetable frantically runs.

In the chaos of chase, they find their fun,
A riot of laughter, the battle begun.
Life blooms amongst the playful strife,
In this patch of green, oh, the joys of life!

Nature's Buried Enigmas

In gardens lush, a tale unfolds,
Of secrets buried, brave and bold.
A gnome in dirt got stuck in place,
With worms debating his funny face.

The rose exclaimed, "I smell a rat!"
While daisies giggled, sat on that.
A riddle posed, a puzzling plight,
Why's the compost dancing at night?

A beetle dressed in purple pants,
Sang silly songs, a wiggly dance.
To find the root of all this cheer,
You must recount the rhymes you hear.

So when you dig in soil so rich,
Beware the giggles, it's a switch!
For nature hides more laughs than woes,
In every wrinkle, humor grows.

The Quagmire's Quandary

Amidst the muck, a frog in flops,
Complains of socks and slippery hops.
He lost a bet on muddy ground,
Now dances where the gunk is found.

A snail creeps by, with style so slick,
Dragging its home, both swift and thick.
"If only I had wheels like you!"
Said Frog, while pondering what to do.

The pond's reflections, quite a show,
What mysteries lurk in waters slow?
The algae swayed with laughter keen,
As fish played pranks, so sly, unseen.

Oh quagmire deep, your secrets stacked,
With jokes galore, let's not hold back.
For every splash, there's fun in store,
Just dive in deep, and find out more.

Life's Everso Fragile Thread

In shadows thin, a whisper flows,
Of fragile threads that dance in rows.
A spider spun, with glee she hummed,
"Who knew this could be so much fun?"

A cricket joined with silly tunes,
While fireflies made sparkly balloons.
Their fiber dance, a woven cheer,
As ants marched by with cakes to share.

Each strand a laugh, a twist of fate,
Brought all together, wouldn't wait.
They laughed so hard, they started to sway,
And nearly lost the night's ballet!

So tread with care on threads so fine,
For every giggle forms a line.
In nature's weave, the joy is thread,
Where laughter twirls and dances spread.

The Cryptic Life Beneath

In the earth lies a party unseen,
With critters laughing, crisp and clean.
A mole who never learned to dig,
Played hide and seek — oh what a gig!

Beneath the surface, chaos reigns,
As veggies joke about their pains.
"Why so sour?" a carrot cried,
"Because I'm buried — what a ride!"

An earthworm wiggled, giving tips,
On how to dance with muddy flips.
The radishes rolled in splendid glee,
As roots exchanged their tales with me.

So if you squat and search the ground,
You'll find the humor all around.
For nature speaks in giggles, friend,
In cryptic ways that never end.

www.ingramcontent.com/pod-product-compliance
Lightning Source LLC
Chambersburg PA
CBHW071651220426
43209CB00100BB/250